MW01144697

THE
VOICE
WITHIN

PAMELA J. OLYNEK

Tellwell Talent
www.tellwell.ca

ISBN
978-1-77302-667-1 (Paperback)
978-1-77302-668-8 (eBook)

Let it be known that this book is based on my personal beliefs and my life events.

-Pamela

DEDICATION

I would like to dedicate this book
to my children and grandchildren.

I thank each of you for all the love and joy
you have brought into my life.

May the concepts in this book inspire
and bless your life as it did mine.

CONTENTS

OPENING PRAYER

Dear God in Heaven and Angels of Light,

Please be with me now as I embark on yet another writing journey. How honored I am to be here once again. You have had me write before. What a joyful task. I am eager to begin. You have promised me assistance every step of the way. I thank you for that. Please guide my thoughts, words and actions throughout this book's unfoldment. May it be your wisdom and your great Love that fills the pages. May I feel your hand on my shoulder as I choose the journal excerpts to share and the channeled writings. May my ego and the desire to control step aside. May I instead allow the flow of this book to carry me along. May I be a clear channel to hear your guidance through each and every stage of this creation process. May this book be all that You would have it be Father. May it find its way to the readers whose hearts are now open to receive your messages. May this book bring hope, encouragement and faith. Most of all Father, may it inspire your readers. May they feel your Presence. May they turn the last page feeling an ever stronger connection to You, the Source of all life. May they choose to walk this Path, one filled with gratitude, joy and wonder. May this book have shown them how to see your Presence in each and every new day.

These are the things I pray for Father, as I embark on this glorious journey with You.

Amen.

INTRODUCTION

Something magical and wonderful is available for each and every one of you. It is the opportunity to live your life in a state of joy and bliss at all times. Step away from living in a state of worry, stress, guilt, shame, anger and any of the other negative emotions. They accomplish absolutely nothing. They only fill your mind, body and ultimately your soul with disease. Why take all the fun out of life? Do you want to reach the end of your life, looking back, only to find a few happy moments? Or do you want to look back over your life and reflect on only a very few troublesome times? Even these can be filled with blessings. Something good can come out of every hurdle. We have only to shift our perception of the circumstances to find it. This book is an invitation to embark on a journey of discovering a new approach to life. One that brings more peace, more joy, more love.

First, let me share with you a little about my life. I was born in Alberta sixty-four years ago. For most of those years, I was lost, alone and afraid. I may not have admitted that had anyone asked me. For the most part, it was as if I was unconscious. I was not in a touch with my true Inner Self. In fact, I had no idea I had one.

Each of you does too, by the way, have an Inner Self, Higher Self, Divine Self. The adjective used is not that important. What you will come to understand through this book, is just how important your recognition of this Inner you is.

Like most birth families, the dynamics in mine had unhealthy aspects. I came out of it a very troubled, lost little girl in a young woman's body. I went from one unhealthy relationship to another, looking for love, peace, comfort, in all the wrong places. I made a lot of poor choices.

Besides trying to fill this emptiness within with male companionship, I also had addiction issues. Throughout those adult years, there were times when I either was sent to a counsellor or chose to see one. I was unable to function in my day to day life. I was having problems with anxiety. I took stress leaves from work at various times.

Gradually, I began to initiate my own search for understanding. What was going on in the inner recesses of my mind that was triggering these bouts of depression? Overtime, I began to seek out more unconventional healing methods. Versus psychiatrists, I would go for hypnotherapy sessions. After that I took some Reiki classes. I felt so much better after this energy work that I soon became passionate about regular sessions. I also added in acupuncture and craniosacral therapy. I went to self-growth workshops. I began to explore different churches. I read self- help books. I began to understand that I was more than the circumstances in my life. I began to believe that life can be more. I was tired of constantly struggling with addictions and the stress of unhealthy relationships, Gradually, I got to the point of being strong enough to leave behind all of it and start over. I was now in my fifties. I got my own place. It was time for me to learn about who I was on the inside. It was also time to provide for myself.

What I discovered is another way to approach life, a path that brought more joy, fulfillment and peace into my daily existence. Read on and discover the components of this new life.

CHOOSING THE SPIRITUAL PATH

I invite you to take the focus off the struggle and strife of daily existence. Keep an open mind. Read what I have to share. I believe we are here to grow and learn as spiritual beings. We are having an earthly experience to evolve our souls. This can be done within a joy-filled existence. It need not be through pain and suffering. We are here to embrace life fully, manifest our dreams, share our gifts and allow the miracles of life to flow to us effortlessly. 'How does one do this?' you may ask. Walking the spiritual path embraces many concepts. I will touch briefly on some of them in this book.

At the top of the list is developing an attitude of gratitude. This in itself can change your life to a more positive experience. Start seeing the blessings in your circumstances.

Next, shift from feeling a victim in your life, to taking full and complete responsibility. Where you are now is a result of your choices. If you made some poor ones, now is the time to make some better ones. This will create for you a brighter future.

Self-confidence, trust in one's self is a vital ingredient. Developing this is a process that occurs one step at a time. A good place to start is keeping one's word to others and more important, to one's self. When you say you are going to do something, whether it is arriving somewhere at a certain time or taking a step towards a personal goal, do it. Keep your word. This begins the road to self-confidence and self-trust. Within each of us is a seed that is meant to grow and blossom into a beautiful lotus flower. That occurs as we grow and evolve into all that we are meant to be. Just as a garden needs the right condition to prosper, so too our lives can provide the conditions for us to grow and blossom. If we are embroiled within addictions for example, our progress in this life is greatly hindered. One becomes stuck on the continuous treadmill the addiction demands. For some, years go by before they find their way off that cycle. For others, it can be an entire lifetime. What is wanted and needed is to fill that inner void with this spiritual path. As famous author Wayne Dyer often writes, we can either live our life as through we are alone or we can choose to acknowledge a God presence. We can walk with Him. I choose, as can you, to believe that within each of is a Divine Light, a spark of our Creator. God placed that within each of us. This part of God that resides within is like an inner compass that can help guide the direction of our lives. Some call this our Inner Self, Higher Self or Divine Self. As I said in the introduction, the adjective one uses is irrelevant. What is vital however is that one comes to recognize that this Higher Self does exist. What the spiritual path entails is listening to this Higher Self versus the lower ego self. By doing this, one will soon discover that stress, worry, guilt, all the negative emotions fall away. Instead one's mindset becomes filled with peace, trust, joy and faith. One will develop this over time. This spiritual path is a chosen way to walk through life. It is a journey that one chooses to embark on. This begins and gains momentum when one has it be in the forefront of one's life. It can no longer be on the back burner as something you will get to 'when you get around to it.' The riches of this Path will be unable to flow your way until you shift your priorities.

When one starts living with a new attitude of gratitude, life changes. Keeping your word and acknowledging you have a

God self within, assists in this positive transformation. These steps cause the energy field around one to rise. It is when one is living their spiritual path that good is then able to be magnetized back into your existence. I have written more on this in the next chapter.

It is time to stop playing victim in your life, whether it is victim to substance addictions, victim to your circumstances (which you created), victim to unhealthy relationships. What it is is no longer important. There is no more blaming the outside world. It is not about a job you hate, friends that you criticize behind their back, being in debt or any of 'that stuff.' Living life that way offers no opportunity for good to come in. You have closed all the doors unknowingly.

Hence, the reason for this book, to show you, in simple terms, a better way. Life is meant to be joyful, magical, and abundant. Heaven is here on earth. It only involves a shift in one's perception.

It is also important for you to understand that you are not alone on this journey. That too is a choice. We live on a planet of free will. Available to us, are spirit guides, who want to assist. We only have to ask them.

Through the gift of prayer, we are able to reach out for help as we walk this spiritual path. My experience has shown me that every prayer is answered. We have only to be mindful to be aware of the response.

We have an excellent guidance system built right within us, as the title of this book states. Ask within. Listen with your heart. Avoid intellectualizing. Instead see the blessings and opportunities.

It takes courage to grow, to choose this spiritual path. Each of us has that courage. In fact, we intuitively yearn for this path.

We feel the emptiness of our lives. We yearn for more. At first we often look in all the wrong places. We can stop now.

Moving forward, means leaving the past behind. It also means forgiving ourselves and others for past grievances. Then letting it all go. This too is a process. It happens over time. With commitment and focus, it can be done. Forgiveness is a necessary ingredient on this Path. We have all experienced pain caused by others. It is time to move forward. It is time for a happier more joyful, peaceful life. This requires us to open our hearts. This is the only way.

The term 'expanded consciousness' applies here. Walking this Path means viewing life with a new perspective. This results in a higher vibration in one's life. The result is expansion, transformation. You are no longer your old self. Life is different. You are different.

When we choose to walk this spiritual path, everybody wins, your friends, your family, your co-workers, your neighbours, everyone. This new way of relating to yourself, to your life is a gift to all. Positive choices and heart filled responses create ripples of joy out across the planet. Each of us makes a difference every day in the experience of our life as well as others.

I have said the greatest gift I can give my family is to be the best I can be. This means doing the necessary work. This may require some of you, like me, to seek the assistance of a professional counsellor. You will need to open closets in your past that require clearing, healing, understanding and releasing. Only then can more joy and peace come in.

One of the biggest steps along my path was learning to love and accept myself. This is a vital ingredient. We must get to the point, in a deep inner level, where we find ourselves truly worthy of all the abundance and prosperity life has to offer.

Self-worth, self- acceptance and self-love are all crucial. The good news is these are gifts you will receive as you walk the spiritual path. It begins with grasping that within us is a Divine Self. We are created by God. He loves us. He walks beside us every day. These truths become a part of your self -concept. This will create a shift in your life to a Higher ground. Rejoice! As you learn to pray on a regular basis, and develop an attitude of gratitude, a relationship beings to develop between you and your Higher Self. Gradually, your intuition becomes stronger, clearer. You begin to listen. Before long, you will also act on that intuition. Positive results will occur. Soon you are praying and asking for guidance in all areas of your life. Now even more joy has an opportunity to enter.

Are you starting to get the picture? Can you see the possibility available here? Life is meant to be a joy filled experience. Are you ready to get started on creating yours? I recall now what my father-in-law said as he lay dying. "It's not about money, is it Pam?" "No," I replied. He was realizing that he had spent his entire life on the 'wrong track.' Do not let that happen to you. You can choose different today!

I shall mention too that another important aspect of this spiritual path is self-discipline. Keeping your word to yourself, as I mentioned earlier, will reap the reward of self-trust. Along with this, will be the achievement of personal goals. Stay focused. Practice self-control. Be self-disciplined. These will result in a life of beauty, peace, health and harmony.

Set achievable goals. Make solid 'baby' steps. This brings results. One does not rush this path. Walk with patience and tranquility, knowing solid progress is being made. This is the way to successful transformation.

I am going to conclude this chapter with single sentence statements describing the 'old' me and then the 'new' me. These statements will outline a brief summary of the daily path I used to walk and the path I walk now.

The Old Me

First thing in the morning, I have a cigarette.

I dash out of the door. It is time to get to work.

I stop for coffee and a muffin.

I smoke, drink and eat on the way.

My first stop after work is the liquor store.

I have already smoked on the way home.

I have been at the same job for twelve years. No career growth took place. No focus.

I get home. I sit down with drinks and cigarettes at the kitchen table.

I eat much later in the evening. Food has no value to me. It is not a priority.

My spouse arrives home. He joins me at the table.

By this time I am on my third drink and sixth cigarette.

I only move to go to the washroom.

Hours go by.

My daughter comes and goes.

So does my life.

Eventually I start to have anxiety attacks.

I take a stress leave from work.

I see a psychiatrist.

I feel lost, scared and alone.

Alcohol is a depressant.

I drink. I take pills.

I have blackouts.

It feels like my husband's focus is all about my appearance.

Customers at work come in just to see what shoes I am
    wearing, or what wig or what outfit.

I became all about the outer shell.

I live years of struggle amidst unhealthy relationships.

Why? Because I am unhealthy so that is what I attract –
    unhealthy men.

I have no boundaries.

I have no self-worth.

I have no peace.

My Life Today

I wake up before the alarm.

I do a morning guided meditation.

I do a crystal stone body layout.

I get ready for work in a tranquil state of mind.

As I drive, I state my intention for the day.

I listen to uplifting, positive music.

I have a positive, harmonious and productive day, just as
I intended I would.

I have a great job with wonderful people.

I was in the right place at the right time to secure such a
glorious position.

There is laughter and joy in this workplace.

I have plenty of room to grow and develop in my career.
I do so.

I feel blessed, fulfilled.

I go for nature walks on my lunch breaks.

I say grace before I eat.

I choose healthy, balanced meals.

I pray often.

I engage in creative pursuits.

I embrace my children and grandchildren with love.

I am now a positive influence in their lives.

I love my life.

I love my self.

I am at peace.

ENERGY

Everything is energy. Our emotions are energy. Our thoughts are energy. We are energy. We live in an energetic force field. What we put out comes back. If we think positive thoughts, positive things happen. If we focus on a negative outcome, a negative result is what we will get. When we form pictures in our mind, day dream, we are giving those pictures energy every time we see it in our mind's eye. So be sure you are 'seeing' what you want versus what you don't want. This is very important.

Let us say you have an upcoming test to write. What you want to do then is to focus on doing well. See and feel your-self writing the test with confidence and success. This adds power to your outcome. What you do not want to do is put any thought at all on failure. It simply is not an option. Failure does not exist as a possibility in your mind set. Understand? It is a very basic principle. Like attracts like. You put out good. Good comes back, like a boomerang.

The more a person is able to maintain a positive emotional state, the more Light-filled energy they hold and create. The result is a happier, more fulfilled life. So focus on the good in life, in you, in others, in circumstances, in everything. This focus, these thoughts are creating your world. Choose them carefully and consciously. Take notice of your think-ing process.

Next, take a good look at your belief system. If you believe you cannot draw. Guess what? Stick men is all you will ever do. If you believe you are going to have a rough day at work, you will. If in your mind, you hate your job, you will no doubt have a bad day. If you say you cannot get along with your coworkers, guess what? That will be what happens. You create your experience through your chosen beliefs. It is all up to you. Spend time on this. Uncover your underlying belief systems. You may not even be aware of them.

Here is an example: 'I never have enough money.' Keep saying this. Continue grumbling those words every day. Lo and behold, what is your result? 'You never have enough money.'

Next, let us imagine this scenario about relationships. Pretend Tom is your healthy boyfriend. Yet you are always saying to your friends, 'Tom takes me for granted. I am so sick of it.' You believe this. You act as though it is true. So guess what? In 'your' world, your boyfriend always takes you for granted. Why not choose a different perception? Shift your thoughts. Shift your experience. 'I love my boyfriend. He is always considerate of my needs. I am really grateful to have him in my life.' Now for the next three months, focus on all the good parts of your relationship. You will soon be dancing on the stars with happiness. What have you got to lose? Give this a try.

A good place to start is to pay attention to your language. Do you use mostly negative words? Lousy, poor, incapable, unable, inadequate, cannot, will not, won't, are examples. Are you critical and judgemental of others and yourself? Are you afraid all the time? Life is meant to be a positive experience. Only that which is for our Highest good wants to flow to us. However, this cannot and will not happen if your energy field around you is one of darkness. This is what happens when you unknowingly live a fear-based life. It is only when you shift your thoughts, language and beliefs to a Higher more positive format that positive things can come in. By doing that, you will have opened the door of possibility to receive back your Highest good. Give it a go. Start today.

One of the key things, in my own life, that helped me stop the cycle of depression was shifting my inner dialogue from negative to positive, from critical to supportive. Disciplining myself to do this was the first step towards a better life. I learned to be aware of how self-critical I was. I noticed the negative language I used towards myself, about myself, I learned over time to change this. I gradually became my own best friend. I started switching to positive self-talk. My inner dialogue became supportive and encouraging. You can do the same. Start now.

Learn to use affirmations. These are positive statements. I am strong. I am beautiful. I love myself. I take good care of myself. I highly recommend Louise Hay. Reading her books can assist you in understanding this life changing concept.

When driving, we turn on our signal to let other drivers know our intention is to change lanes. In the same context we can set our intentions for the day, for that job interview, for a relationship, for our health. You want to be in the driver's seat of your life. You want to be setting daily intentions. This will assist you in creating positive results. If you want to have a more fulfilling life, implement this concept.

Every day on the way to work, I say aloud in my intention for my day. I describe how I am going to have a joyful, harmonious day. I state that my day will be productive, efficient, effortless and go by smoothly and quickly. I also daily reaffirm my chosen beliefs. 'I am always in the right place at the right time doing the right thing for the Highest good of all, myself included.' I continue, 'I always make all the right choices in both my personal and professional life for the Highest good of all, myself included.'

I also add in how much I love my job and the people I work with. I connect with that love as speak these morning affirmations. I thank God for my job. I see it as a blessing in my life. I often carry on, thanking God for my car, the clear dry roads and for the brand new day. I pray too, that I do my part on the highway to keep all of us safe.

Do you get the idea I am presenting here? It is all about our mind set, the thoughts we are choosing. Ninety-nine percent of the time, I do have a fabulous, joyful, productive and effortless day. I also travel safely.

I was introduced to Reiki many years ago. I was seeing a hypnotherapist at the time. She was helping me resolve blocked childhood issues. This practitioner was also a Reiki Master. She ran a school for teaching others this healing method. I decided to register for the first class to get my Level 1 Reiki.

That class is forever etched in my memory. It was an incredible experience. My initiation into working with Reiki Energy was profound. I have been a regular participant of Reiki most of my later years.

Reiki is, in simple terms, about opening up to receive Universal Energy. Then one allows this to flow in, either to yourself or through your hands to your client. I love receiving the benefits of Reiki. I recommend energy work to assist you on this spiritual path. Participating in such healing modalities accelerated my transformation. I am now able to allow myself to live a happier, more fulfilling life. I strongly recommend readers to explore this further. Reiki raises one's vibrational energy, allowing you to be a match for more positive experiences to flow into your life.

I have chosen to include here part of a journal entry from October, 2012.

'Last night I was blessed to receive a different type of energy session. This one is called Ill Activation and Universal Sphere. First of all let me say that I deliberately started a body cleanse about five days prior. As well, I renewed my exercise program. I continued my hour daily walks in nature. I wanted to raise up my vibration. I also had an acupuncture session the day before this energy work. Interesting enough, the acupuncturist chose to do a layout that balanced my heart with all my energy centers. This particular type of session is about assisting the individual in living more from their heart, their true center.

Prior to my meeting for the energy work, I did, as I always do, which is to set my intention for the session. I also said a prayer. I prayed that the Ascended Masters would be there to assist the facilitator and that the session would be one of Light and Love and for my Highest Good. I prayed that the session would be blessed in God's honor and in the name of Jesus. During the day at work, I made an extra effort to stay hydrated. I ate lightly of healthy food. I affirmed I was opening up to this healing session, opening up completely every part of me, to allow in what was being offered. I was consciously preparing myself to be an open channel to receive.

The session itself took about thirty minutes. There was no touching of the physical form, unlike Reiki. Rather, the facilitator worked in the energy field that surrounded my body.

She worked in such a way as to shift my human makeup to create a new 'setting' as it were. While on the table, I definitely felt the presence of different entities. It reminded me of a Reiki session I had in Golden, B.C. While on the table with the Master Reiki practitioner beside me, I felt the definite presence of other beings all around the table. This evening now was similar to that only this time, I could also see their shadows as they moved about on the left side of the room. The practitioner was working on the right side.

As we shared at the end, she said that her channeled guide is always present on the opposite side of the table from her. The guide was similar to a High Priestess who, during her time on earth, was a healer. I could feel this guide working over my body. I focused, in a meditative way, to be totally at one with the sound of silence that surrounded me. Next, I could sense myself off to the left side, behind this presence. I was able to observe as they worked over my human form. I liked being out of my body and watching from a distance. I focused on keeping my mind in the meditative state that allowed me to do this. The presence explained to me that the work and changes it was doing was so I could live my life the way it was 'intended' that I would.

I was very grateful for what was happening and for this incredible opportunity. I silently gave thanks frequently throughout the session.

I am reminded now that I also, in the session, experienced that we are always surrounded by love. I can now always tune into that love energy field. We are to live in joy. When we do that, we naturally are where we are supposed to be. We then attract into our lives only that which is for our Highest good. When we live our lives doing what brings us joy, we are in harmony with our true essence, which of course is love. Our vibration is then up. We naturally attract more good to us.'

We have an inner guidance system to assist us in making choices. This is our feelings. Before I make any purchase for example, I ask myself, 'How do I feel?' as I am holding that one item. Everything has an energy field. We can tune into that. Then pay attention. You will know immediately if it feels right. If I feels positive and good inside while I am holding the item then I know it is a wise choice to purchase it.

Once you have been on this path awhile, being consistently in tune with your Higher Self, you can add in this simple technique. You bring your thumb and index finger together at their tips forming a circle. Next, do the same thing with your other hand. Now interlink them forming a chain affect. Put the store item under your arm and ask questions. "Should I purchase this? Is it for my Highest good?" Pull your two arms apart. If your link holds solid, that is a yes. If it is weak, that is a no. I use this method often.

Observe your life and the lives of those around you. What do you see? Pay attention. Have you ever made the connection between the day you handed back to the cashier the extra five dollars she gave you by mistake and the compliment your boss gives you for a job well done? You help a neighbour take a heavy load to the dump with your truck. The next day a shop keeper cuts you a deal on a large item purchase. Notice this 'flow' in your life.

Hand in hand with this, be mindful of what you say. Listen to your words. 'I never get to work on time.' 'I'm always broke.' 'I never get a break.' 'I'm too fat, too poor, too ugly, too short', whatever else you want to put in there. The point is these statements are creating your experiences. Ask yourself, 'Is this statement what I want to be true in my life?' If not, change it.

Once you decide to pick new statements, work on 'believing' them. Idle words have no power.

One that I recently worked on is shifting out of fear based thought to 'Aren't people great! Everyone is so kind to me. Aren't people amazing! Everyone is so wonderful.' Guess what? Now my experiences of people are great and wonderful. It is important to focus on what you want. This applies to loved ones as well. See your family healthy, happy. See them successful, fulfilled. Avoid chatting with people constantly about their diseases, struggles, money problems, and so on. By doing this, you are keeping them focused on their negative perception of things. Instead bring joy into their life. Take your daughter second hand shopping when she is struggling with money issues. Have your son over for apple pie making when he is out of work. These are examples from my own life. We can be a vehicle for helping others to shift their focus from the negative to the positive. This then allows uplifting energy a chance to flow into their lives.

One thing that can be a definite stumbling block on the spiritual path is unresolved issues. The best thing you can do to speed up your shift from negative energy existence to a positive happy one is to forgive yourself and others.

Positive energy cannot flow into your life, for example, if you have not talked to your brother in the last five years. Whatever the initial disagreement was, get past it. Your happiness, your life depends on resolving this. Your forgiveness can be a gift to those involved. How they respond is their choice however.

Just as important is forgiveness of one's self. You must fully let go of mistakes you have made. We all have these in our past.

The thing is to not ruin the rest of your own life because of them. Pay any necessary dues. Make peace within. If possible meet with those involved. Clear the air. In doing so you are removing energy blocks that are very likely impeding your progress.

Everything has energy. This includes your home environment. Energy needs to flow. Remove the clutter. Get your cupboards organized. Throw out that cracked Tupperware, those old worn out shoes and the clothes that no longer fit.

I had been holding onto a pair of runners way past their expiry date. Recently, I finally took the big step. I put them in the garbage.

I had been looking for a new pair all to no avail. A few days after I tossed the runners, I was in a store for something. I was instead 'guided' to the shoe section. Guess what? I finally found a pair that fit comfortably. I am a walker. Proper footwear is imperative. I was so happy. 'Just goes to show,' I said to myself, 'Let go of the old so the new has space to enter.'

Fill your living space with beauty. Surround yourself with items that make you feel uplifted, positive. Get out family photos. Put on the counter that special gift. Whatever room you enter, you want to feel happy and secure. Put out items that initiate such feelings.

One area I had to work on is to stop saving the new for later. I would buy new shoes, new clothing. They would sit in my closet too good to wear, same with nice candles, special china and other items. I finally got to a place on this spiritual path where I realized my life is happening right now. It is not a future event. I now embrace my treasures immediately. I suggest you do the same. Keep this new energy flowing.

Start paying attention to the music, the lyrics you listen to, the movies, TV, you watch. Keep them positive, uplifting, even inspiring.

I love Karen Drucker's music. Her lyrics are empowering. I choose inspiring movies often based on true stories.

Pay attention to the company you keep. Are they deeply embroiled in the cycle of addictions? Are they manipulative and controlling? Do they always have to be right? Are they quick to anger? Do they constantly find fault with you? If you replied yes to any of these, you may want to leave these people off your contact list. Surround yourself with positive people, ones who see the good in life and in you.

Manifestation is an area I have been working with in my own life for several years. The key concepts are outlined by the authors in my recommended reading list.

"And whatever things you ask in prayer, believing, you will receive." (NKJ Matthew 21:22)

We create our own life by the words we speak, the thoughts we think, the beliefs we have. This ability to put into our life what we want is ours to choose and to develop.

For example, I have used these principles to get the car I wanted, the job I desired, the apartment I live in. Now on the way is the healthy relationship I deserve.

By focusing on what you want, by believing you deserve it and can have it, by acting as if you already do have it, these are all necessary tools to this creation process. When you are energetically of the same vibration as what you desire, the object of your focus will appear. Using the aforementioned tools will assist you with this outcome. Remember, this only will occur as long as what you want to attract into your life is for the Highest good of all. The item will show up in God's timing not yours. He knows your needs better than you. For example, my perfect job did not show up until I had made a necessary move and had a much needed holiday.

Love is energy. Love is eternal. Death is a doorway. Your deceased loved ones have only changed form. They still exist. When we 'feel' our love for them, we stay connected to them. They receive that love energy. They have the opportunity to send it back, providing you are open to receive it. This is based on our beliefs.

Here is an excerpt from a journal entry I wrote last winter.

'I had just the most amazing experience. I saw and felt my dad. He was wearing his yellow jacket that he used to wear when putting around the garage and yard.

I had been doing some leg exercises in front of the large glass sliding door. I looked out. There he was! Tears filled my eyes. I thought, "Oh Dad, I am sorry." He replied, "No regrets sweetheart. It is the relationship we have now that matters."

Tears continued to flow as I clutched my hands to my heart. "Tears of joy Dad, tears of joy." I whispered aloud.' I have had many such experiences with both my deceased parents. My journals contain numerous entries where I have felt them close. At times, I am guided to a special place to find a meaningful symbol of their presence, their love. I open my heart and receive their gifts. I say a prayer, thanking God for

His Inner Voice that led me to the precise spot to receive this magical wonder.

I have decided to end this chapter with a journal entry from July 2012.

'When I am at a higher vibration, I am more likely to experience positive life occurrences. We achieve such a higher vibration by living our day to day life as that of being on the Ascension Path. This means we focus more on our spiritual Path that our worldly one. We eat healthy foods, exercise, spend time in nature and have an attitude of gratitude. We use positive words, engaging in only positive thoughts. We have our relationships in order. We have completed with our past. We have no unresolved issues. We take total responsibility for our life. We understand the Law of Attraction (refer author Ester Hicks.) We know we are the creator of our own life. We understand that love is a vibrant energy force, one that surrounds us and every living thing. We meditate on this. We 'feel' it and align with it. We draw it forth for others in our prayers. We visualize this energy force surrounding people, events, and our world. In this way, we are making a difference. 'My dear Pamela, this journal entry is a reminder also for your ears. So often, we hear your heartfelt prayers that you are yearning to make a difference, for your life to matter. You have only to realize that every single day that you live your life in the way that you just described, you make a difference just by the positive energy field around you. This affects everyone that is a part of your day. This happens whether they are in your physical space or in your thoughts and prayers. Your energy field is emitting all day long these positive love centred waves. They go outward like a ripple over a pond. They are a positive benefit for all.'

SIGNS

Walking this spiritual path has taught me to open my eyes, my ears, my heart, so I can receive 'signs.' It is important to be aware of our surroundings. We are to take note of possible signs and their messages. I often refer to this activity as 'connecting the dots.' Paying attention to the 'bumper cars' God has placed on my path is another aspect of this spiritual walk. Let me explain.

My belief is that when doors of opportunity open effortlessly, those are the ones we are supposed to enter. If we knock on a door (analogy) and we meet with resistance, we are best to reconsider our choice. We then proceed to the next door and the next until a door does open effortlessly. This particular door and the opportunity within it, inevitably turns out to be for Highest good. I call these closed doors God's bumper cars. They keep us from making the wrong choice. This concept reminds me of the bumper pads young children use on bowling lanes.

An example occurred this past fall. I was planning my annual holiday out to Vancouver Island. I was unable to connect with my oldest son. I had called numerous times. I wanted to confirm the date for my visit. When I went to book accommodation where I usually stay, they were full. I called another place. They also had nothing available. I stopped and took notice. I said to myself, 'Okay something is going on here. Between no accommodation available and my son not responding, I am obviously not to be at that specific area of the island on those dates.'

I emailed my friend where I was to have some energy work done. We made some logistics adjustments. I listened to my Inner Guidance system. I called for accommodations at another location with different dates. I was able to complete a booking within minutes effortlessly. When I later arrived, I saw clearly what an incredible gift it was that I was booked at this particular site. The place was absolutely perfect for my post energy work.

Pay attention to those 'road blocks' and to your Inner Voice. Stop. Tune in to how you are feeling. If it does not feel right, rethink your choices. I have even felt nauseous at times when extreme situations are a definite red flag 'no.' A few years ago, a particularly bad dream kept me off the highway. This prevented me from being involved in a serious accident. I thank God for sending that 'sign.' I have also had upsetting dreams about family members. These dreams get my attention. They are telling me I need to go and see how my family is doing. My ensuing actions have a positive impact on their lives. Our daily world is full of opportunities to receive these messages and their guidance. They are gifts to us.

I just came in from doing an errand. At the store what first caught my eye was a plaque that said, 'Listen to your heart. It knows where it is going.' I had been struggling with a decision. Here was my answer. Also in this store, I felt 'guided' to turn down a specific aisle. Low and behold, there was sunflower dish. This is one of my signs that my mother is delivering a Heaven sent, 'Hello.'

A few years ago, I was on my way to work. As I took the ramp from one highway to join up to the next highway, I glanced back over my shoulder. I saw a huge angel cloud in the sky! Later that morning, I received a call from the care facility where my dad resided. He was dying. I needed to get there as soon as possible.

I also do not believe in coincidences. Striking up a conversation with a stranger, missing your bus, stopping at a specific bulletin board, all have potentials to alter the course of one's life. This last one happened to me.

My daughter and I were taking a career counselling workshop. This lasted over several days. She missed one particular day. Being on my own at break time, I took a stretch break. I wandered down the hall. I stopped to read the bulletin board. There was a poster advertising openings in a school program that also included government funding. After class, I inquired. There had just been a cancellation. I had an immediate interview. I was accepted. Life altering circumstances unfolded.
I was meant to walk down that hall on that day. I was 'guided' to stop and read that bulletin board. I was prompted to act on the information immediately. That cancellation was meant to open a door in my life.

When walking this spiritual path, 'signs' often become a daily occurrence. You may also be lead to purchase 'tools' to assist you on your journey. These could be specific books, music CDs, guided meditation CDs, maybe even a specific crystal.

While at the airport this year, I wrote down the title of a book that caught my attention. A month later, I ordered it from the library. The book was a perfect complement to what I was working on at the time.

In conclusion, let me encourage you to pay attention. Where is your line of vision? What does it see? What are your ears hearing? What are you being drawn to do, to be, to say? Life is a miracle. Participate.

DIVINE SYNCHRONICITY

Divine synchronicity happens when we allow choices to be guided by this Inner Divine Self. By doing this, we are able to be in the right place at the right time. Now we can receive the blessings, the gifts God has for us.

Miracles happen to those who believe in them. Trust that Inner voice. It could be as simple as being in the right store at the right time to get a product you need at fifty percent off. I was at a store at the precise time a few years ago. I reconnected with a long lost friend. Wow! Talk about Divine timing!

Open your heart. Let God in. He has so many joyous wonders He wants to share with you.

Recently, I was guided at just the right time to turn my head in a certain direction while driving home. My eyes saw the most beautiful site! It was evening. The town park was all lit up in festive Christmas lights. I circled around the park, fully embracing all of it. How glad I was that I turned my head at that precise instant.

A prism of rainbow colors perpendicular in the sky on a cold sunset was a gift given to me recently. I had left work at the precise time to catch a glimpse of this beautiful sight.

Life is meant to be a glorious adventure. Climb on board. What is your heart saying to you right now? Pause and listen. Does it want you to pick up the phone to tell someone dear that you love them? Does it want you to sign up to be a Big

Brother for a lonely child? Perhaps it wants you to light candles around a hot bath. You are being encouraged to take some quiet relax time for yourself. Pay attention!

When I am out in the car, my vision is often drawn to store signs. I know this is for a reason. I park. I go in. I am intuitively led to an item I have been looking for. Sometimes it is a household item. I have none left. This store has it on sale.

Divine synchronicity comes about through observing the world around us. Be mindful. Be present.

A friend suggested recently that I find a seat at the front. We were attending an evening workshop on crystals. I was being guided (through her comment) to sit at a certain spot. I was drawn to an amethyst crystal that was visible only from that chair. This crystal became a valuable tool in a project I was working on.

A few years ago, a friend called me. She had seen a specific job listing. I took down the number she gave me. I called. It turned out to be the best job for me. It had all the qualities I had been envisioning. I got the job.

These are examples of how important it is to take notice of everything happening around you. There are no coincidences. There are however Divine messages. Listen. Pay attention. Trust your Inner guidance system.
This Inner voice wants to assist you in being in the right place at the right time. You are meant to live a miraculous life.

We are all connected. We are all part of a Divine tapestry. We can also be in the right place at the right time to benefit others. Even in small ways, this can happen.

One day I stopped at the library to renew my library card. From there I was to go to my daughter's place. I renewed my library membership. The staff member gave me my new card. She said, "You no longer need this old card." I hesitated briefly. "I'll keep it for now. The library phone number is on this one." I traveled to my daughter's home. She was in the middle of looking for a library DVD that was due. She could not find it. She needed to call them to renew it. I handed her my old library card with the phone number on it!

Two weeks ago I cashed a forty-eight dollar cheque. It had finally arrived. It was repayment for an error a company had made. Within a few hours, I received a phone call from a family member who needed to borrow forty-five dollars!

We cross paths with other people's lives at specific times for a reason. We are there to teach them. We are there to learn from them. For example, we could be working at the same company at the same time for a while. During that time we could end up supporting each other through difficult times or encouraging each other's creative pursuits.

Divine synchronicity, Divine timing is able to occur more frequently in our life when we walk the spiritual path.

The Universe supports us when we are taking action steps for the Highest good of all. Several years ago, while at work I was guided to look at the job postings. There was one in Victoria, British Columbia. I was qualified. I applied. A phone interview was arranged. It went well. While I waited for their decision, I started to pack. I took action as though I had already received the response I wanted. I had often dreamed of living on the west coast. I had a son who lived near Victoria. I needed to leave an unhealthy relationship. Unexpectedly doors began to open to make this move possible. Now was the time for me to actually do it. The Universe was telling me loud and clear. Of course, I got the job. All the logistics for the move were handled quickly and efficiently. I was in the right place at the right time to receive this Divine blessing. How grateful I was!

I will end this section with a journal entry from December 23, 2016.

'Today, while doing pre-Christmas errands, I had a craving for butter tarts. In my mind they go with Christmas. I was no longer in the city so to find gluten free ones in my home town could be a challenge. I tried several stores, was about to give up, when my Inner Voice popped into my head the name of a store. I was driving by my street, still debating to just go home. I asked within and received confirmation. 'Yes,' I was to still carry on to the store. This surprised me, yet off I went. Soon enough, I found some butter tarts and at a great price. They were not gluten free. That was okay I decided. Just as I was about to leave the store, I saw Ed. He was the husband of Edith. Edith and I used to work together. As I walked to my car after a brief chat with Ed, I suddenly realized why I was 'guided' to this specific store. My deceased parents' names are Edith and Ed. With tears of joy and gratitude, I acknowledged their Merry Christmas greeting. By listening to my Inner Voice, I was able to receive their 'Hello from Heaven.'

This incident reminds me of other times when I am prompted from within to go to a certain location. I later discover that was not my real reason for being there. I believe that sometimes God plants a seed in our brain. He knows this will motivate us to take necessary steps. He wants us to be at a certain place at a specific time.

I encourage you to trust, have faith and go where you are led. God has gifts for you. Open your heart. Receive them.

FAITH AND YOUR INNER VOICE

Faith is the most valuable tool to take with you on this spiritual journey. Faith is developed over time, like a muscle, with consistent workouts. Just as physical fitness is a valuable asset, so too faith can see us through challenging times.

Drawing on developed faith keeps one from succumbing to life experiences with emotions of despair, fear, doubt. How does one develop this faith? Faith is built on our beliefs.

'I am always safe and protected.'

'That which I need, flows to me.'

'I am guided from within on all my affairs.'

'God loves me and wants only the best for me.'

These are examples of affirmations I use regularly. They express my beliefs. What are your beliefs?

One character trait that can assist one's faith is to develop accountability. Keep your word to yourself and others. Keep commitments you make to yourself. Even the simple things, like when you say to yourself, 'I am going to complete this task by the end of week.' Do it. Over time you will learn that you can count on yourself. I highly recommend the book; The Four Agreements (refer the book list).

Another important ingredient is opening up your heart to the concept 'There is a God.' There is a Divine Source. This Divine Being loves you. God wants what is best for you. There is no reason to be afraid. Hand in hand with this realization is acknowledging that you are a spiritual being. Fear is an illusion which keeps you from enjoying your life journey.

Gradually over time, as you learn to live with an attitude of gratitude, you will soon start receiving more blessings in your life. This in turn develops hope and belief that life can be good. It can be a positive experience. Ever so gradually, as more and more things start going your way, you start to believe that 'Life Is Good.' Then when a 'down' time does come along, you notice you are handling it better. 'This too shall pass.' 'Something good will come out of this.' These are two affirmations I use.

Our faith is also strengthened when we listen to our Inner Voice, then act on it. We each have access to this Inner wisdom. We have only to listen. The more we pay attention to it, the clearer it becomes. Soon that Inner Guidance is available quickly and effortlessly.

We will get 'promptings' to do something. We may not understand why. I have learned over time to act on those 'promptings.' Trust them. They always have a positive outcome. I tell myself I do not need to understand everything. God knows the bigger picture. My job is to trust this Inner Voice and act on it. This is easier to do when your belief system supports the spiritual aspect of life. Here are some examples.

One Sunday recently I was sorting through Celtic music CDs that I no longer listen to. My Inner Voice was nudging me to take them into work and give them to a specific co-worker. It turns out she loves Celtic music. She was surprised and pleased at this unexpected gift.

A few months ago, I called up a Reiki practitioner I know to see if she could book me in for a session later that day. I discussed with her if she would be agreeable to accept a crystal bowl for payment. I was listening and acting on my Inner Voice's nudging. What would she say? Well she did have time available to see me that day. Also, she had been wanting a crystal bowl. She was thrilled at my offer to have this gift be her payment for the Reiki session.

When we trust and act on this Inner Voice's guidance, everyone wins. Through us, God can uplift others. Following through on this Inner Guidance is an act of faith. God placed this inside each of us to bless our lives and those around us.

You will know it is your Inner Voice talking because it 'feels' right. It 'feels' good. You may even feel excited at the prospect of following through on it. Trust these feelings. You are being Divinely guided.

Another thing I am grateful for happens after I walk away from a completed task. I may have been at a store or at work or planning a holiday for example. I am barely finished when I hear within, 'You made all the right choices.' 'You did the right thing,' is another phrase I frequently hear. My Inner Voice is reassuring me that I listened to my Divine guidance system correctly.

Intuitive guidance can be very subtle. A thought flashes across your consciousness.

Here is a recent example. I was opening up the kitchen blinds. My Inner Voice said softly, 'Put those two plants back in the bedroom.' I immediately knew it was so they could get the afternoon sun. Instead of acting on this, I left for work. Later, the clouds cleared. The sun was out bright all afternoon.

Here is another example. I was about to purchase new face cream. I was determined to try a new one. My Inner Voice said, 'Don't get this one.' I did not listen. I discovered after a few uses my skin definitely had a reaction to this particular cream.

When these incidents happen, I allow them to be a blessing. 'See Pamela,' I say to myself, 'Your Inner Voice is always right.' Whenever I find myself beginning to worry about others, I pray for them and then for myself. I do the latter because worry solves nothing, helps no one, accomplishes nothing.

My answered prayer back, brings me comfort and peace. I am told to remember that they too are God's children. He loves them. He walks along beside them even if they are not aware of this as yet.

I pray that God will lay His hand upon their heart and their circumstances, may He comfort them. I am told to trust their life journey. It has its own unique unfoldment. I must stand back and allow them to experience the consequences of their actions. It helps me too, when I reflect on my own past. I made it through those dark times, so will they.

These concepts will give you faith when you are concerned about loved ones.

There may also be times when you are prompted to do something for another. It may not even make sense to you. Do it anyways. Trust that God knows what they need. Be honoured He is using you to assist. It could be as simple as giving a stranger a compliment.

As you witness consistent successful outcomes, your faith in your Inner Voice will grow. Soon you will be confident enough to take more risks and follow even bigger promptings. Be glad. Rejoice at this wondrous gift God has given you!

A Poem by Pamela

My life unfolds effortlessly
Moment by moment
Divinely perfect in every way.
I know this to be true.
I trust this to be so.
I surrender and let my life flow
Rejoicing with gratitude
As I do so.

ANSWERED PRAYER

I began this book with prayer for I have learned that every prayer is answered. When we pray with all our heart to a God we truly believe in, we are heard. We are answered. It is the flow of life. Prayer is sending energy out, so an energy response must flow back. This is where tuning into and developing one's intuitive self is valuable.

It is important to be mindful, to be present. Notice when a book falls off a shelf, a truck passes with a slogan, a billboard sign, an overheard conversation. All of these can hold the response to your prayer.

Now I am not talking about prayers like, 'Lord give me a million dollars.' That is not a prayer. I am talking about a heartfelt 'talk' with God. These are real prayers.

The first important ingredient is belief. The next is faith. First, believing there is a God. Second, faith that He loves you, cares about you. As authors of books retelling their near death experiences explain (refer to book list) God is real. Heaven is real. Now I am not talking about the old traditional sense of pearly white gates. I am talking about an all-encompassing peace, love and Light. There is a Universal Energy, a Divine Source, a Creator of all.

I especially like the analogy author Anita Moorjani uses in her book Dying To Be Me. It is like we are living in a huge warehouse. As humans we see only what our flashlight illuminates. Once we die, we leave our human form behind. Now, in spirit form, we can see the entire warehouse. It is as if someone turned on the light switch. There is so much more going on than we realize.

Just because we cannot see something nor measure it scientifically, does not mean it does not exist. Walking this spiritual Path requires one to have an open mind as well as an open heart.

Prayer is a gift. It provides us the opportunity to stay connected to our Creator, this Divine Energy Source. We also have access to the assistance of spirit guides, angels and Ascended Masters. We have only to ask. This is essential for they cannot assist us in our journey otherwise. We live in a universe of free will. They are not allowed to intervene unless invited (except in life or death situations before our time.) I will add here that it is necessary to specify 'Angels of Light' when you are inviting in spirits to assist you. You can distinguish a helpful Light-filled spirit guide by its loving and supportive voice, offering insight and gentle guidance. Author Doreen Virtue is an excellent source on this topic.

Along with prayer comes saying grace at every meal. This simple act of bowing one's head in gratitude for your meal can work wonders in uplifting your vibrational energy field. Herein is an opportunity to align with who you truly are, a spiritual being. Thank God for your food. Have a conversation with Him. Thank Him for your day. Set your intention for your evening. Bless those around the table with you.

Keep connected to Divine Source. Allow yourself to know you are loved. You are not alone on this journey through life.

No heartfelt prayer for another human being is ever wasted. All prayer in earnest is heard. I pray frequently. I invite you to do the same.

For example, pray for the stranded motorist on the side of the road. Pray for the family on the news who lost a loved one. Pray for the boy walking alone in the cold with no hat or gloves. Pray for the people the ambulance is rushing to assist. We send out Light-filled energy when we pray. Now is the time when our world needs it more than ever.

I have here a journal entry of mine from May 2016.

'Best day ever! Out with grandson. Stopped at lake. Saw a mother duck and her ten baby ducklings resting on a weed bed. Then we saw a muskrat. On way to the car later we saw the duck family in the water. Went back later with camera. Couldn't find them. Saw baby geese this time. Aidan and I had a great day playing catch, playing basketball, floating popsicle sticks. What a gift it is, this relationship, grandma and grandson.

Thank you Father for answered prayer. As I drove to pick up my grandson, I prayed that it would be a joyful day, celebrating life, celebrating our relationship. You brought into our day the miracles and wonder of new life, the baby ducks and the wonder of Your loving creatures, like the muskrat. You filled our hearts with joy at the splendour of life itself.'

This next example of answered prayer occurred just this past week. I had an idea that involved my daughter. I prayed about it to God. I asked Him to lay His hand upon the situation. I shared that I trusted Him to let me know whether it was a good idea for all involved.

I was so excited about the prospect that very soon after my prayer, I was dialing my daughter's number. The phone rang and rang. No answer. I started to think maybe this was not such a good idea after all. She called right back. In that short break of time, I had reflected on this more. By the time I answered her call, I had a backup conversation in place. The second 'sign' came when she was interrupted on the phone with a family upset. She had to say goodbye immediately.

I had my 'answer' to that prayer. Circumstances prevented me from presenting my idea to my daughter. God was telling me my idea was not for the Highest good of all.

Next, I would like to share with you two 'channeled' entries from my journals.

This first one is from July, 2015.

'Your concern for your children is valid. Earthly journey is a challenging experience especially when travelled without spiritual awareness. Your continual prayers however do assist.

It is also important for your own well- being that you do indeed surrender 'their' burdens to God and His angels. Inviting them to assist your loved ones, offering to be a vehicle of assistance, yes these things you can do and do do. Yet more than that Pamela dear you cannot do. For their lives are their choices same as your life is a result of your choices. They are adults now and must bear the consequences of choices not thought through just as you have had to do.

Trust God to watch over them and do all He can. For it is a free will universe. The children themselves would do well ask us for assistance for we are the Angels of Light as you so graciously call us.'

This next one is a part of a 'channeled' entry from December 2015.

'...It is true however that addictions slow down this process as you well know yourself, Pamela. Reflect a moment. See your own acceleration once addictions were left behind. Let us remind you again dear one not to stand in judgement nor responsibility for another's progress. This is up to them. Go forth now in peace into the day trusting that their Guardian Angels are forever by their side...'

After praying, it is important to apply the 'Let Go Let God' principle. Surrender any worry or concerns into His hands. Know that He has heard you. Trust that His answer is on its way. Keep in mind; this will happen according to His timing not yours.

Remember that God sees the bigger picture. We may not agree with His answer. Often, the further unfoldment of affairs reveals why He responded as he did.

I should mention here that God does not cause car accidents, nor does He create disease. He does however help us through the tough times.

It is just as important to thank God for His answer. Let Him know you are appreciative of His guidance and His love. Be grateful.

'When a believing person prays, great things happen.' (NCV James 5:16)

WORDS OF ENCOURAGEMENT

I want to make it clear that developing a relationship with your Higher Divine Self can greatly assist you on your life journey. Trust those Inner promptings, that Inner Voice. It is from your Divine all-knowing Self.

Your outside circumstances are an indication of how you are doing inside. Some parts of your life may be good, others in a sad state of affairs. These are clues as to what you need to work on. The goal is to restore balance and harmony in every area of your life. Do the work. Throw out the weeds from your inner garden. They are detracting from your well-deserved joy-filled life.

When you walk this spiritual path you are always given what you need when you need it. This is providing of course that what you are up to is for the Highest good of all.

Like today, for example, I needed my car attended to. Lo and Behold, I had just become a member of AMA (Alberta Motor Association). After a brief wait, I was able to have one of their trucks come out and boost my car so it would start. I had also recently established a connection with a garage within walking distance of my home. I called first thing this morning. The owner put my name down on his wait list. A call came in later. He was able to fit me in today!

Another example is when I got my key stuck in the apartment building entrance door. I had to leave it there, go upstairs and call the locksmith. He was having his lunch and would be along in a bit he said. I prayed for help. Then I surrendered the situation to God. Before the locksmith arrived, there was a knock at my door. My neighbour from down the hall stood there. "Is this yours?" he asked. In his hand was my outdoor key in perfect condition. "Thank you so much," I said. "You also saved me a fifty dollar locksmith fee."

To assist the flow of good in your life, pay attention to your thoughts, feelings and language. **Keep** them **positive and grateful.** What you say, what you focus on is affecting your future. The Bible says, '...for whatever a man sows he will also reap.' (KJV Galatians 6:7)

You will bring your life into a more harmonious state by walking this spiritual path. Soon you will be a Light for others. Your relationships will improve, becoming more fulfilling.

Remember, you are not alone. The spirit guides and angels are here to assist you. You have only to ask. They will however only assist with those situations that are for the Highest good of all.

As you develop a more positive attitude with an open grateful heart, your life will become easier. To accelerate your journey even more remember to add the following ingredients. Take full responsibility for all aspects of your life. Practice self-discipline. Say good-bye to holding grudges, being angry, blaming others.

Energy work can be a valuable catalyst for positive change. Reach out to practitioners of the different healing modalities. Seek help with the 'tough' stuff.

Energy work can assist you in releasing any blocks you may have to a joyful, abundant life. You may feel unworthy. You may be afraid of change, of the unknown. There could be unresolved traumas stuck in your body.

Reach out for assistance. It is time to let go of the fear. Allow the real you to shine.

Addictions will impede your progress. They will also hold you back from fulfilling your life purpose, which is to walk this spiritual path. Be willing to let go of those self-soothing attachments. You do not need them. You only 'think' you do. Shift your mindset. Reclaim your Inner power. You are wise enough and strong enough to achieve any goal.

Kneel in prayer. Ask for help from addiction centres. They helped me.

By embarking on this spiritual Path, you open up to the possibility of a life without addictions. The concepts outlined in this book will provide the motivation to release these old behaviour patterns. Your Divine Self will assist you in choosing this healthier more rewarding lifestyle.

I want to remind you that you are not alone. Spirit Guides and Ascended Masters are waiting to assist. They want to walk this Path with you. This is their purpose. Open your heart, believe and invite them in. **You shall receive.** Just be sure to ask for help from Beings of Light.

A Channeled Message

'Love and Light
Surround you now
Forming a beacon
For all above to see.
Shining so bright
That others may benefit
Throughout this coming day
And week.
In this small yet
Significant way
Our planet's vibration
Is raised.
Never ever belittle
Your part
My dear
For as you know
We are all connected.
We, the Angels & Archangels
Say thank you
For inviting us in
Every morning
During your meditation.
Just as you feel honored and blessed
So do we.
Keep doing what you are doing
My child.

You are on the right Path
For the unfoldment
Of your skills and gifts
To assist in this planet's
Evolution.
You are not alone.
We will be assisting
All of you
Who are willing.'

Many authors have shared their journey that others my benefit from what they have learned. Explore the recommended reading list at the end of this book.

Do not despair nor be discouraged when you hit a rough patch. Remind yourself it is part of the process. You are healing. Be thankful for that. Stay committed to your journey. Understand that whatever is going on is for a reason. It will bring you further along your Path.

I believe that those of us who come from the darkest of pasts shine the brightest on our spiritual Path. We have been lost, felt the pain, the guilt, the shame. We persevered through all the steps. Our past made us stronger, within ourselves and in our faith.

A Channeled Message

'You are a miracle
Of Love and Light
In so many ways
On so many levels.
Mother Mary walks by your side
Each and every day.
Those tears that want
To burst forth
From the depths
Of your heart
Are indeed voices
Of your entwined souls.
So do not run
From those tears
Nor push them back down
In your human
Minded determination
To be strong.
Rather embrace them
And their song.

As you proceed further along this Path, eventually the Divine synchronicity I spoke of earlier will happen more frequently. Events in your life will start lining up on their own to support you. Seize these opportunities. They hold blessings for your progress.

When we choose to walk this Spiritual Path everyone wins.
When you do the work required for your walk to be successful, everyone wins.
When you forgive yourself and others, everyone wins.
When you start loving yourself, opening your heart and listening to your Inner Voice, everyone wins. This means your children, your spouse, your parents, your siblings, your coworkers, your neighbours. This means all of humanity.
We are all connected.
When you choose to walk a Higher Path, you benefit all of mankind.

Remember, on this Spiritual Path, you are developing your connection to your Inner Voice. Your Inner guidance system is strengthened. More incidents of you being in the right place at the right time for the Highest good of all, occurs. You become a positive ripple in the lives of many. You show commitment to your spiritual evolution by walking this Path. Therein exists the opportunity to inspire others to do the same.

A big challenge for me as I walk this Spiritual Path is learning to open my heart again. I share this here for I am certain I am not alone in this struggle. So many of us have to learn to trust life again, to trust people. This is not always easy.

Learning to trust myself was an important step. Along with that, was developing a positive self- concept, self- image, one that was based on my beliefs this time, not someone else's. Over time, I learned to love, support and encourage myself. I learned to be my own best friend. After all, I am my companion through life.

I discovered I had an Inner Self whose purpose was to guide me through this life, that my experience would be a joyful one. I learned there existed a God Source, a Universal Energy that also loved me, supported me and walked beside me. I was not alone. I gained comfort and strength in that. I still do. Gradually, I was able to open my heart, to allow myself to feel again, to let people in. My heart continues to expand.

I have learned that Love is the greatest energy force of all. I know my life changed forever the day I let God into my heart. I also know that within each of us is a part of this God. His Inner Voice is our saving grace.

It is a gift. Embrace it. Use it to assist you in transforming your life. You are meant to have a peaceful, abundant, joyous one.

God Bless You,

Pamela

CLOSING JOURNAL ENTRY

My purpose in sharing this entry is for you to hear just how important it is that we each walk this Path. It benefits not only us and our families but all of humanity.

OCTOBER 2012

'Our intention in bringing this 111 Activation and Universal Sphere forth is to assist in raising the consciousness of many people. This will result in a raised vibration of the entire planet Earth. This will restore her to her original state of magnificence. We hear your prayers Pamela. You see the beauty and wonder of God's creation with all the earth's splendours.

This last quarter of 2012 is particularly important. That is why we need your full attention now and of many like you. We need to move forward quickly to reach the intended goal for this time period in this millennium. That is why when in the labyrinth you were asked Pamela if you were willing to make the commitment necessary. You answered, 'Yes.'

So now, here we are with you, ready to work alongside you, as you continue on your chosen Path. This is and always will be your true 'work.' This Path Pamela, this process, is what will make the real difference for which you have been praying. You and many others (and there are many of you) shall walk through this process, achieving and living your lives more and more from this new 'expanded consciousness.' As a result, the vibration of the entire planet will be raised. Then you truly will see great and wonderful changes occur.

This is your 'important work' Pamela. You have been praying to be of service. This is your opportunity. We are here to assist you in every way. Like a ripple in the pond, each one of you, as Light workers, will have a tremendous effect on the whole.

This journey of yours Pamela, just as you have been saying all along, is indeed the best gift you can give your children and grandchildren. Never for one minute, think that you are not doing enough. You have prayed and prayed to be of service. This is your answer back. By you participating fully in this process that has now been initiated by the 111 Activation, you will achieve your intention to be of service.

So hold your head high Pamela Joan and know that what you are up to in your life (and have been for some time now) is indeed life changing for all.

Thank you for this Channeled Message. Thank you indeed!'

We can together transform any remaining darkness on this planet into Love and Light. Each one of us matters. Each one of us makes a difference. Remember too, that once we choose this Path, we will receive all the 'Ascended' help we need. We have only to ask for it in prayer.

EPILOGUE

I live a magical life
Full of awe and wonder
Every day.

I am so blessed, so very blessed.
The Angels of Light
Guide me every step of the way.
My journey reflects this.

Years of commitment
To this spiritual Path
Have now reaped the rewards,
With this peaceful heart
And eyes for beauty.

Thank you Father
For this brand new day
That I am able to experience
It all once again.

RECOMMENDED READING LIST

Listed here are authors whose books assisted me on my spiritual path. I especially enjoyed the audio books of authors Wayne Dyer, Louise Hay, Ester Hicks and Rhonda Byrne. Hearing their insights and wisdom in their own voice adds power to their message. Keep in my mind some authors also have DVDs, and meditation CDs. I have only listed here a title or two. <u>Please also explore the authors' other publications.</u> Enjoy! Expand! Evolve!

Beckwith, Michael – *Your Life Purpose*

Browne, Sylvia – *The Other Side and Back*

Byrne, Rhonda – *The Secret*
                                The Power
                                The Magic

Canfield, Jack – *A Book of Miracles*

Cooper, Diana – *Enlightenment Through Orbs*

Curteis, Eileen – *Reiki: A Spiritual Doorway to Natural Healing*

Dyer, Wayne – *Wishes Fulfilled*
                           Power of Intention
                           Four Pathways to Success
                           Excuses Be Gone

Eadie, Betty – *Embraced By The Light*

Gawain, Shakti – *Creative Visualization*

Hay, Louise – All of her publications

Hicks, Ester and Jerry – All of their publications

Holmes, Ernest – *This Thing Called You*
The Science of Mind

Jordon, River – *Praying for Strangers: An Adventure of the*
Human Spirit

Katie, Byron – *Loving What Is*

McVea, Crystal – *Waking Up In Heaven*

Millman, Dan – *The Laws of Spirit*

Moorjani, Anita – *Dying to be Me: My Journey from Cancer to*
Near Death to Healing

Pearl, Eric – *The Reconnection*

Richardson, Cheryl – *The Unmistakable Power of Grace*

Ruiz, Don Miguel – *The Four Agreements*

Sharma, Robin – All of his publications

Virtue, Doreen – *Signs*
Angel Words
Saved by An Angel

Walsh, Donald Neale – *Conversations With God*

Yanzant, Iyanta – *Living Through the Meantime*

GUIDED MEDITATION CD LIST

Asar, Justin Moikeha – *Crystalline Activations: St. Germain:*
The Violet Flame
Isis & Osiris: The Octahedrons Of Light

Fairchild, Alana – *Mystical Healing*

Godwin, Karina – *Living & Embracing Your Abundance*

Halphern, Steve – His Subliminal CD Series

Hay, Louise – *Self-Esteem Affirmations*

Highstein, Max – *Visiting Angels*
Visiting Mother Mary

Large David – *Spirit Guides*

McStravick, Summer – *Flow Dreaming* (book and CD)

Richardson, Cheryl – *Tuning In*

Virtue, Doreen – *Chakra Clearing Meditation*

MUSIC

I highly recommend Karen Drucker. Her lyrics are filled with positive affirmations and language.

CPSIA information can be obtained
at www.ICGtesting.com
Printed in the USA
LVOW11s1225070517
533187LV00001BA/1/P